WOMEN IN S.T.E.M

Women Who Changed Science and the World. Pioneers in Science, Technology, Engineering and Math.
6-12 years

Sumita Mukherjee
www.wizkidsclub.com

More books from WIZKIDS CLUB:
Stem/Steam Activity Books: 6-10 Year Kids

COOL SCIENCE EXPERIMENTS FOR KIDS

Grades: 1-5
Skill level: Beginner
Time: 19 projects; 30-40 minutes each

COOL SCIENCE EXPERIMENTS FOR KIDS is an amazing book full of hands-on activities. With awesome Science, Technology, Engineering, Art and Math project ideas, it is an easy way to entertain any bored kid! A great way to acquire 21st century skills and STEM learning.

Inside this book you will find projects on Simple Machines, Merry-go Round, Spinning Doll, Exploding Bottle, Safe Slime, Architecture, Crafts, Games and more!

Loads of fun with projects that burst, glow, erupt, spin, run, tick and grow!

FAMOUS STEM INVENTORS

Grades: 1-5
Skill level: Beginner
Time: Reading time: 15-20 mins and activities of 20-30 minutes each.

FAMOUS STEM INVENTORS introduces kids to the world's most famous young inventors in the field of S.T.E.M. (Science, Technology, Engineering and Math). All things that we enjoy are a product of brilliant minds, scientists and engineers. This book imparts information that is interesting and engaging to young boys and girls between 6-10 years of age.

STORY OF INVENTORS: Kids will be transported to the fascinating world of famous creators and learn about their first inventions: Glowing paper, Popsicle, Windsurf board, Television, Earmuffs and more. The book arouses their natural curiosity to be inspired from their role models.

DESIGN PROCESS: It showcases the Engineering Design Process behind every invention. Highlights what they invented and how they invented, thereby, revealing the steps to all new discoveries.

SKETCHING AND DESIGNING ACTIVITY: It encourages kids to sketch and design their own ideas through the design activity. This book prompts kids to think creatively and it arouses their natural curiosity to build, make and tinker.

STEAM AHEAD! DIY FOR KIDS

Grades: 1-5
Skill level: Beginner
Time: 21 projects; 30-40 minutes each

STEAM AHEAD! DIY FOR KIDS is an amazing book full of hands-on activities. With awesome Science, Technology, Engineering, Art and Math project ideas, it is an easy way to entertain any bored kid! A great way to acquire 21st century skills and STEM learning.

Inside this book you will find projects on LED cards, dance pads, handmade soaps, bubble blowers, Play-Doh circuits, cloud lanterns, scribbling bots and more!

Awarded 5 stars by READERS' FAVORITE site, Parents, Educators, Bloggers and Homeschoolers.

JOIN THE WIZKIDS CLUB TEAM!

The WIZKIDS CLUB features Highly Engaging Activities, Experiments, DIYs, Travel Stories, Science Experiment Books and more!

Visit www.wizkidsclub.com today!

🌐 www.wizkidsclub.com

Author: Sumita Mukherjee
Illustrator/Designer: Lester D. Basubas

Table of Contents

Introduction

When you think about experts in fields like science and engineering, there's a good chance you'll picture someone like this:

Science, Technology, Engineering and Mathematics are often seen as 'boys subjects' and a bit, well, stuffy! You might be surprised to learn that many of the things we take for granted today like the windscreen wiper and some of our essential medicines, were, in fact, invented by women. In this book, we're going to take a look at - and celebrate - the achievements of some of STEM's largely unsung heroines from the last couple of hundred years as well as a sneak peek at some modern STEM stars such as Lisa Kudrow and Lady GaGa.

Without science, technology, engineering and math our societies would still be living in the dark ages - literally. Science allows us to light our homes, power our factories, treat and cure illnesses and much much more. Few of us are lucky enough to have been untouched by cancer, whether ourselves, or a loved one and, many more lives would be shortened and lost if not for the work of Marie Curie.

Technology is more and more important to our societies as it continues to move forward with breakneck speed. So much of life today is governed by computers and technology - from life saving medical care to instant communication across the globe. When we think about movers and shakers within the world of technology, names like Steve Jobs, Bill Gates and Marc Zuckerberg instantly spring to mind but, many technological advances have been the handiwork of women.

Timeline

There have been many hurdles for woman to pursue the sciences. They have remained predominantly male with historically low participation among women.

Scholars are exploring the various reasons for the continued existence of this gender disparity in STEM fields. Those who view this disparity as resulting from discriminatory forces are also seeking ways to redress this disparity within STEM fields. Some proponents view diversity as an inherent human good, and wish to increase diversity for its own sake, regardless of its historical origin or present cause. Not having access to the universities and not being paid a fair wage are just a few of those barriers. Let's celebrate the milestones in history and accomplishments woman have made in education and science.

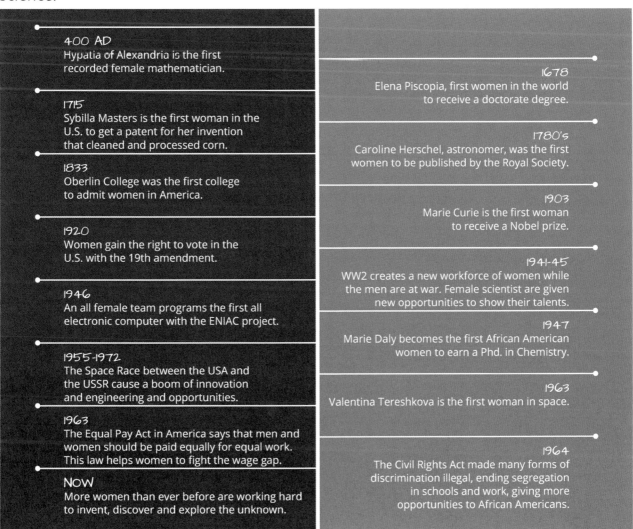

400 AD
Hypatia of Alexandria is the first recorded female mathematician.

1715
Sybilla Masters is the first woman in the U.S. to get a patent for her invention that cleaned and processed corn.

1833
Oberlin College was the first college to admit women in America.

1920
Women gain the right to vote in the U.S. with the 19th amendment.

1946
An all female team programs the first all electronic computer with the ENIAC project.

1955-1972
The Space Race between the USA and the USSR cause a boom of innovation and engineering and opportunities.

1963
The Equal Pay Act in America says that men and women should be paid equally for equal work. This law helps women to fight the wage gap.

NOW
More women than ever before are working hard to invent, discover and explore the unknown.

1678
Elena Piscopia, first women in the world to receive a doctorate degree.

1780's
Caroline Herschel, astronomer, was the first women to be published by the Royal Society.

1903
Marie Curie is the first woman to receive a Nobel prize.

1941-45
WW2 creates a new workforce of women while the men are at war. Female scientist are given new opportunities to show their talents.

1947
Marie Daly becomes the first African American women to earn a Phd. in Chemistry.

1963
Valentina Tereshkova is the first woman in space.

1964
The Civil Rights Act made many forms of discrimination illegal, ending segregation in schools and work, giving more opportunities to African Americans.

WOMEN IN
SCIENCE

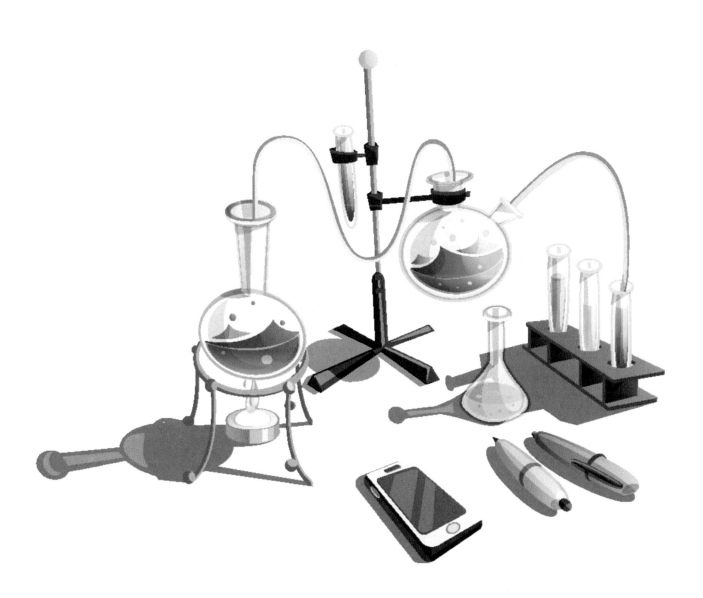

1) Marie Curie : Scientist 1867 to 1934

Maria Skodowksa was born in Warsaw in 1867 to a very poor family who could have no idea as to who their fifth child would become.

During her work as a governess, Maria developed a passion for learning and, in 1891, she joined her sister in Paris in order to attend university there, reading physics and mathematics at the world famous Sorbonne. When the young scholar married scientist, Pierre Curie, she not only took his surname but changed her Christian name to the French spelling of Marie. Along with her husband, Marie began working as a researcher at the School of Chemistry and Physics and, it was here that their pioneering work on uranium began. Inspired by the work by Professor Henri Becquerel, the couple were fascinated by the way that the chemical's invisible rays were able to pass through solid matter and generate electricity.

Through tireless research and experimentation, the Curie's managed, in 1902, to isolate radium as radium chloride, despite the ill effects on both of their health. This work would eventually lead to the discovery of the benefits of radioactivity in the treatment of cancer and other illnesses. Despite the tragic, accidental death of her husband in 1906, Marie's work continued and, she was rewarded in 1911, with a second Nobel prize.

FUN FACT:
Marie's notebooks are still considered so dangerously toxic that, today they're stored in lead-lined boxes, and will likely remain radioactive for another 1500 years.

During the first world war, Marie put her talents to use to develop a small mobile x-ray unit which could be utilised on the battlefront. Until her tragic death from radiation poisoning in 1934, Marie continued her research, winning many more prizes and, to-day, she is most famous for the excellent medical facilities which bear her name.

Few of us are lucky enough to have been untouched by cancer, whether ourselves, or a loved one and, many more lives would be shortened and lost if not for the work of Marie Curie.

2) Caroline Herschel: Astronomer 1750 to 1848

German astronomer, Caroline Herschel first planned on a very different career - as a singer! At the age of 22, Caroline moved to Bath in the South of England to train in music but her interests soon took a very different direction.

Along with her brother, William, she developed a passion for the night skies and shelved her musical ambitions in order to become William's assistant as he strove to create effective lenses with which to view our universe. The first woman to ever be paid for scientific employment, Caroline, along with William, recorded around 2500 new nebulae and star clusters. This work formed the basis for the New General Catalogue (NGC) which is still the official body for naming the stars in our skies.

FUN FACT:
Herschel was only 4 feet 3 inches tall— her growth was stunted due to typhus when she was 10 years old.

In addition to her work with her brother, Caroline discovered 14 new nebulas, eight comets and, added a staggering 561 new stars to Flamsteeds catalogue.

3) Barbara McClintock: Geneticist 1902 to 1992

Nobel prize winner, Barbara McClintock, dedicated her life to the study and analysis of maize.

Although the study of corn may not seem like a vital contribution to society, Barbara discovered that the genetic makeup of the plant provides an incredible amount of valuable information. Through her research into maize, Barbara discovered the existence of jumping genes - sequences of DNA threads which are able to travel between the genomes.

Although her work was initially dismissed as worthless, Barbara persevered and was eventually able to prove that jumping genes may be able to determine which of the genes within cells are 'switch on' which was an undiscovered method of recognising the difference between cells.

It was later suggested that jumping genes may make up around 40% of the human genome, all due to Barbara's studies and, some 40 years before a formal study was commissioned, she also introduced the concept of epigenetics whereby genes are altered in response to certain external factors.

FUN FACT:
Barbara was also the first scientist to fully understand and outline the centromere and its role in genetics.

In 1983, Barbara was awarded the Nobel Prize in Physiology or Medicine.

4) Dorothy Hodgkin: Chemist 1910 to 1994

A former teacher, Dorothy Hodgkin was known for being teacher and advisor to former British Prime Minister, Margaret Thatcher, but her achievements were so much more than that.

Despite a lifelong battle with arthritis, Dorothy was tireless in her work to understand and improve on the world of medicine. In her early career, Dorothy was prolific in the field of X-ray crystallography and, through her work, was able to determine the atomic structure of cholesterol, penicillin and vitamin B12. Dorothy's work on vitamin B12 earned her the honour of being the only woman to be awarded the Nobel Prize for Chemistry in 1964.

FUN FACT:
Dorothy, at one time, seriously considered giving up chemistry in order to pursue a career in archaeology.

In later life, after vastly improving x-ray crystallography techniques, Dorothy dedicated herself to mapping the structure of insulin which would become a life-changing advance for diabetes sufferers around the world.

5) Rosalind Franklin: DNA Scientist 1920 to 1958

It's impossible to overstate the importance of our understanding of DNA and Rosalind Franklin was a vital part of the process, despite being largely unrecognised for her work. Referred to by her biographer as 'Dark Lady of DNA', Rosalind's work was constantly undermined by others in the industry.

Born in London to a wealthy Jewish family, Rosalind studied physics and chemistry at Cambridge University's women's college before going on to employment with the British Coal Utilisation Research Association. During this time, Rosalind was largely involved with the study of coal and its porosity.

In 1946, Rosalind spread her wings and moved to Paris in order to perfect her skills in x-ray crystallography which would soon become her passion. After four years in the French capital, Rosalind returned to London to take up a post with King's College where she was betrayed by her employer and mentor, Wilkins, when he claimed her work as his own as he developed the now famous DNA model.

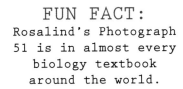

FUN FACT:
Rosalind's Photograph 51 is in almost every biology textbook around the world.

Rosalind continued her work after Kings College and worked on the structure of the tobacco mosaic virus and the coal and virus structure until her tragic death by ovarian cancer at the age of 37.

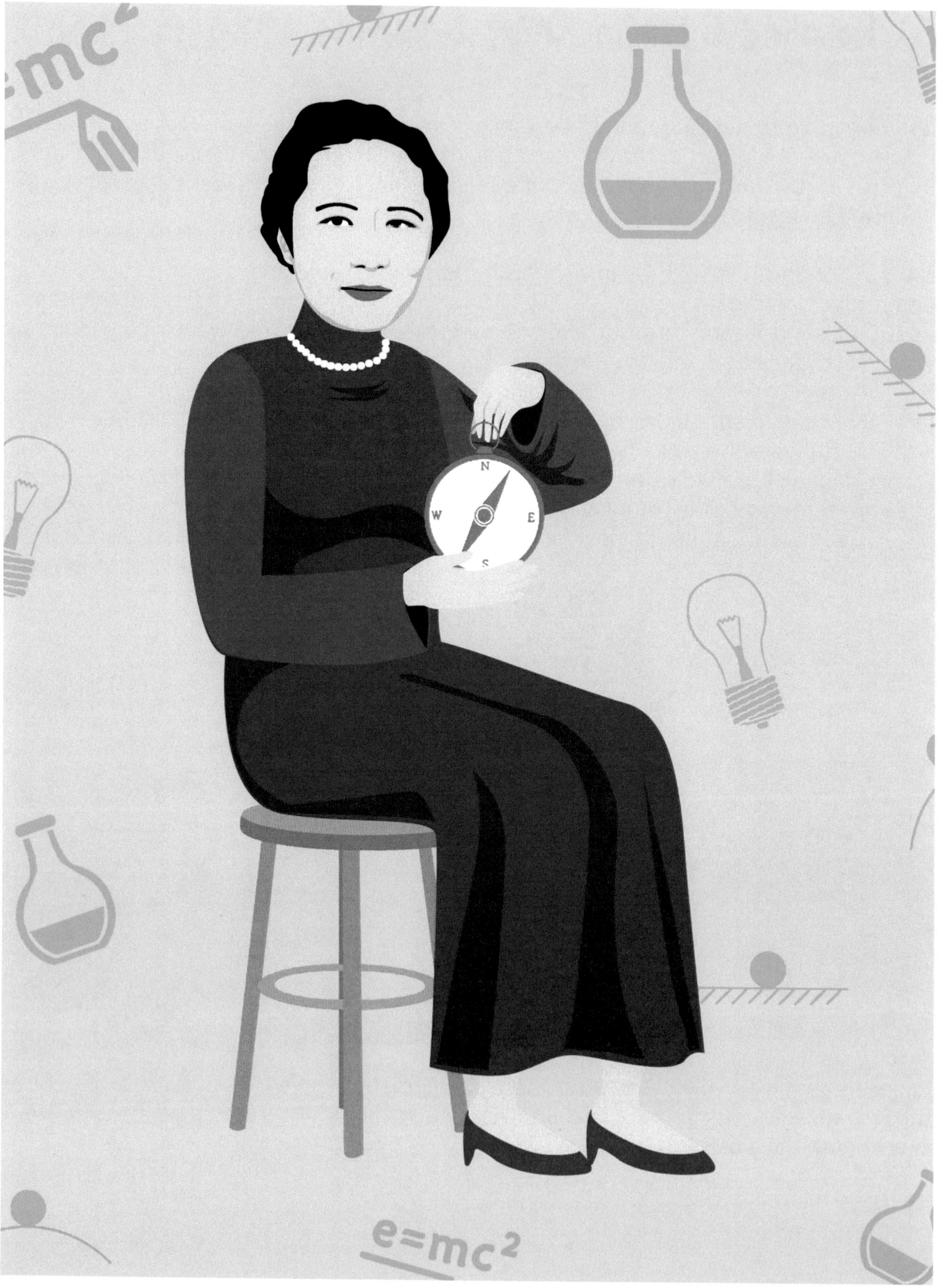

e=mc²
N
W
E
S

6) Chien-Shing Wu: Physicist 1912 to 1997

From an early age, Chien-Shiung Wu was inspired by Marie Curie, the great chemist and physicist who became the first woman to win a Nobel Prize and the only woman to win it twice.

Teaching herself physics from books borrowed from friends, Chien-Shiung graduated from school with top marks in 1934 and moved to the United States of America in order to pursue her passion for physics.

It wasn't long until Wu was being compared to her idol, Marie Curie, in terms of her talent and dedication and, 1944, she was invited to join the Manhattan Project to work on uranium enrichment and radiation detection. Subsequent to this role, Chien dramatically went on to provide a fundamental law of science incorrect, earning her a front page piece in the New York Times.

FUN FACT:
Chien-Shiung had a number of nicknames including the "Chinese Madame Curie," the "Queen of Nuclear Research" and the "First Lady of Physics." Her students at Columbia University called her "the Dragon Lady" after a character in a popular comic strip.

In an incredibly unfair move, in 1954, two of Chien's colleagues were awarded Nobel Prizes in Physics but Chien's contribution went unrecognised.

She was, however, awarded the National Medal of Science and the Wolf Prize in Physics and, in 1990, had the honour of having a star named after her.

WOMEN IN TECHNOLOGY

1) Grace Hopper: Computer Programmer
1906 to 1992

'Amazing Grace' was a mathematician and computer programmer who was one of the first women to ever achieve a PHD.

On leaving school, Grace too employment teaching mathematics but was soon called upon to join the war effort within the US Naval Reserves. During this time, Grace was sent to Harvard University in order to learn how to program the Mark I, probably the first ever functional computer and a passion was born. Little did Grace know at that time that this work - and the navy - would form the rest of her life!

Grace soon discovered a passion for bringing computing to the masses with a vision of ordinary folk owning and using computers on a daily basis. Winner of the Defense Distinguished Service medal and Computer Science Man of The Year award, Grace invented the computing COBOL language and, is also responsible for the term 'debugging' after famously discovering that a moth had disrupted the running of a computer's processing.

FUN FACT:
The Cray XE6 "Hopper" supercomputer at the National Energy Research Scientific Computing Center, or NERSC, was named after Grace.

When she retired in her 80s, Grace was the US Navy's oldest active duty commissioned officer.

2) Hedy Lamarr: Actress and Inventor 1914 to 2000

Best known for her role in controversial movie, Ecstasy, and her tumultuous love life,

Hollywood legend, Hedy Lamarr was also a talented inventor. Every moment of Czechoslovakian Hedy's spare time was spent on her latest ideas and it's said that she successfully streamlined
'Howard Hughes' racing aeroplane.

Her greatest work, however, was an invention which she intended to donate to the US navy during the second world war. Described as a secret communication system, Hedy harnessed the idea of 'frequency hopping' in order to guide radio controlled missiles undetected by the enemy, under water.

FUN FACT:
Hedy was married and divorced six times!

Along with her friend, composer George Antheil, Hedy patented the idea in 1942 and it was subsequently adopted by the military. Despite this, incredibly, Hedy was told that her talents would be put to better use as a pinup and troops entertainer.

3) Ada Lovelace: Computer Programmer
1815 to 1852

Thought by many to be the world's first computer programmer,

Ada was born into English nobility and, on finishing her schooling, was employed by Charles Babbage to document his computer invention - the Analytical Engine - which would never come to fruition due to lack of funding.

Ada had the foresight to see beyond the mathematics of Babbage's invention and wrote what would become the world's first ever computer algorithm.

FUN FACT:
Ada Byron was the daughter of Lord Byron, the Romantic poet, and his wife, Anne Isabelle Milbanke.

Although her work was largely unrecognised during her lifetime, her contribution gained recognition after her untimely death of cancer at the age of 36 and, today, computer programmers celebrate Ada Lovelace Day in her honour.

4) Katherine Johnson: Aeronautics Expert 1918 to Present

One of just three black students chosen to integrate into West Virginia graduate schools in 1939,

Katherine Johnson earned notoriety from an early age. A fairly ordinary career as a teacher took a dramatic turn when an opportunity arose in 1952 for Katherine to take a position at the National Advisory Committee for Aeronautics laboratory in Langley. Just two weeks into Katherine's tenure in the office, Dorothy Vaughan assigned her to a project in the Maneuver Loads Branch of the Flight Research Division, and Katherine's temporary position soon became permanent.

For the next four years, Katherine worked on analysing the investigation of a plane crash caused by wake turbulence but, in 1957, her career took another dramatic turn when she provided some of the vital data for the launch of the Soviet satellite, Sputnik and subsequent space travel projects.

FUN FACT:
Later in her career at NASA, Johnson worked on some of the agency's early plans for a mission to Mars.

In 1962, the orbital mission of John Glenn would put Katherine's name firmly on the map with the construction of a worldwide communications network, linking stations around the world to IBM computers.

Katherine also worked on the Space Shuttle as well as co-authoring 26 research reports before her retirement. In 2015, at the age of 97, Katherine was awarded the Presidential Medal of Freedom by President Obama.

5) Annie Easley: Computer Scientist 1933 to 2011

Two weeks after reading an article and an advertisement for 'human computers', Annie Easley began a career which spanned 34 years.

Despite racial discrimination excelled at running simulations for the newly planned Plum Brook Reactor facility at NASA. When human computers were replaced by the machine variety, Annie adapted easily to becoming a computer programming, using complex languages such as the Formula Translating System and the Simple Object Access Protocol to supply many of NASA's programs.

During this time, she developed and implemented code which was used in the research of energy-conversion systems and was involved in alternative power technology, including hybrid vehicles and the Centaur upper stage rocket.

FUN FACT:
Before civil rights laws of the 1960s, Easley helped train African Americans to take the voting test in her home state of Alabama.

One of the first STEM advocates, as well as her work for NASA, Annie was actively involved in encouraging students to embrace STEM subjects by giving talks on her work with NASA. As well as her impressive career, Annie spent her whole life fighting for equal rights or women and for racial minorities.

6) Mary Allen Wilkes: Computer Programmer 1937 to Present

Although she left the world of technology in 1975 to pursue a career as an attorney, Mary Allen Wilkes was possibly the first person to use a home computer which she had built herself.

Known for her work with the LINC computer, Mary was also responsible for developing the assembly linker model which is still used today in modern programming compilers.

FUN FACT:
Wilkes was the first person to design and work on a computer privately at home in 1965.

A true pioneer in what was a very male dominated industry, Mary made her mark on technology throughout the 1950s and 1960s.

WOMEN IN ENGINEERING

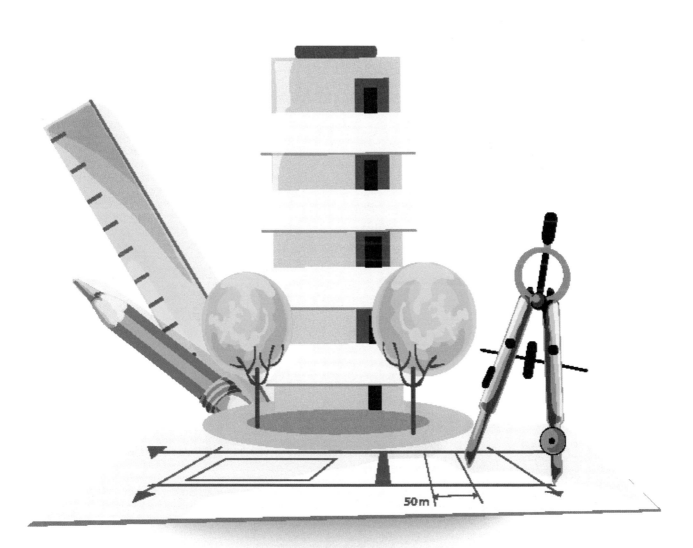

50m

1) Emily Roebling: Engineer 1843 to 1903

When Emily Roebling's husband, Washington, was taken ill whilst working as Chief Engineer of the Brooklyn Bridge, she made the surprising decision to take over whilst he was incapacitated. Emily worked tirelessly on managing the construction and liaising with city officials - as well as caring for her sick husband - until the famous steel and wire suspension bridge was completed.

FUN FACT:
It is said that, during her inaugural walk across the Brooklyn Bridge, Emily carried a rooster with her for good luck.

Emily also became the first person to ever walk across the bridge.

2) Martha J Coston: Signal flare Inventor 1826 to 1904

When Martha J Coston tragically found herself a widow with four children at the age of 21, she would have been forgiven for looking for somebody to help her make ends meet. Instead, after finding plans in her late husband's notebook for a pyrotechnic flare, she decided that she would endeavour to complete his work for him.

She quickly realised that the project posed two major challenges - First, the flares had to be simple enough to use in coded color combinations. Second, they had to be bright, durable, and long-lasting in order to be effective tools for ship-to-ship and ship-to-land communications.

FUN FACT:
Martha eloped with her late husband at the age of just 16

After the war, Martha continued working to perfect her invention and she went on to launch The Coston Supply Company which continued to trade until the late 1970s.

3) Lillian Gilbreth: Psychologist and Engineer 1878 to 1972

Lillian Moller was a scholar who earned masters and bachelors degrees in literature and was working on her doctoral studies when she met her husband, Frank Gilbreth, in 1904. The husband and wife Gilbreth team went on to create time and motion studies in order to increase the production and effectiveness of industrial employees.

The two worked on a number of projects together until, in 1915, Lillian switched her interests to psychology and earned her doctorate from Brown University. She then rejoined her husband, applying her psychology expertise to his physiological insights to produce writings such as Fatigue Study and Applied Motion Study.

FUN FACT:
Lillian's 12 children are featured in the best selling book, 'Cheaper By The Dozen'.

All of this as well as producing 12 children, kept Lillian busy until she retired from teaching at the University of Wisconsin in 1955.

4) Edith Clarke: Electrical Engineer 1883 to 1959

Farmer's daughter, Edith Clarke, was the first woman to be elected a fellow of the American Institute of Electrical Engineers (which became the Institute of Electrical and Electronic Engineers, IEEE).

A former maths tutor, she was employed by AT&T to train a group of 'human computers before going on to take a role as a human computer for General Electric. In 1921, Edith filed a patent for a 'graphical calculator' which was to be used to solve electric power transmission line problems.

From there, Edith moved to Turkey to take up a position as a professor of physics and, on her return, to General Electric in 1922, she became the first salaried electrical engineer.

FUN FACT:
Edith helped build the Hoover Dam, "contributing her electrical expertise to develop and install the turbines that generate hydropower there to this day."

Before her retirement in 1956, Edith returned to teaching - this time at the University of Texas, during which time she received a lifetime achievement award from the Society of Women Engineers.

5) Mary Anderson: Inventor 1866 to 1953

It may be hard for us to imagine now but, before American, Mary Anderson's, lightbulb moment, drivers needed to stop their vehicles and get out in order to clear rain, snow and ice from their windshields.

Spotting this problem, Mary completed a design in 1903 for a device called 'Rain-Rubbers' which was patented in 1905. Mary's Rain-Rubbers were operated by a lever inside the vehicle, allowing drivers to stay warm whilst clearing the windshield. Constructed from a swinging arm with rubber blades, the Rain-Rubbers could be easily removed during times of better weather.

FUN FACT:
After her death, 17 trunks were found in Mary's room which, when opened, revealed a large collection of gold and jewelry which helped with family financial problems.

By 1916, most cars used electrical windscreen wipers based on Mary's original design.

6) Elsie Eaves: Civil Engineer 1898 to 1983

A role model for girls and young women, Elise Eaves was one of the first female civil engineers and a fellow of The Society of Women Engineers.

The first woman to earn a degree in civil engineering from the University of Colorado, Elsie's long and distinguished career included a number of awards and honours and, in 1983, she wrote an article

FUN FACT:
Elsie's construction inventories became so well-known and respected that they became databases for other researchers, including those who needed supporting figures to drive new construction after the Great Depression.

In the June issue of U.S Woman Engineer, highlighting the changes that she had seen within her career and lifetime.

WOMEN IN MATH

1) Emmy Noether: Mathematician and Researcher
1882 to 1935

The daughter of a respected mathematician, Emmy not only inherited her father's talents but also fought her way through sexual prejudice in order to become a renowned leader in her field.

In 1915, Emmy was invited by Hilbert and Klein to explore Albert Einstein's theory of general relativity. Although her talents led her to being offered a teaching position at the university, the objections to a female teacher were so vehement that she was only able to teach and research under Hilbert's name. In 1918, Emmy became known for Noether's Theorem which details the relation between the symmetries of a physical system and its conservation laws.

Following her theorem, Emmy was finally admitted as an academic lecturer under her own name in 1919. Between 1927 and 1933, Emmy worked as both lecturer and researcher and developed a number of new theories.

FUN FACT:
Upon hearing about Emmy Noether's death, Albert Einstein wrote to the New York Times, calling Noether "the most significant creative mathematical genius thus far produced since the higher education of women began."

With the advent of Nazi power in 1933, Emmy and other Jewish lecturers were dismissed from their posts and she subsequently moved to the United States to become a visiting professor at Bryn Mawr College until her sudden death following complications during surgery.

2) Sophie Germain: Mathematician 1776 to 1831

Known for her contributions to the studies of acoustics, elasticity and the theory of numbers,

Sophie Germain, like Elsie Eaves, struggled to make her voice heard due to her gender. Fascinated by numbers as a child, Sophie was inspired by mathematician Joseph-Louis Lagrange who she met at the Ecole Polytechnique in Paris (from where she obtained notes under a male pseudonym) and who became her mentor. In 1809 the French Academy of Science offered a prize for a mathematical account of the phenomena exhibited in experiments on vibrating plates conducted by the German physicist Ernst F.F. Chladni.

FUN FACT:
In 1804 she initiated a correspondence with Carl Friedrich Gauss under her male pseudonym. Gauss only learned of her true identity when Germain, fearing for Gauss's safety as a result of the French occupation of Hannover in 1807, asked a family friend in the French army to ascertain his whereabouts and ensure that he would not be ill-treated.

Sophie submitted memoirs three times but was unsuccessful until she finally won the prize in 1821 with a memoir which treated vibrations of general curved as well as plane surfaces.

3) Julia Robinson: Mathematician 1919 to 1985

Born in St. Louis, Missouri, Julia Robinson received her PhD in 1948 for her dissertation based on 'Definability and Decision Problems in Arithmetic'.

Despite persistent health problems, Julia taught part-time as a professor at Berkeley and, later became known for her affiliation with the decision problem and Hilbert's Tenth Problem which called for an algorithm to figure out whether a Diophantine equation could contain integer solutions. .

Julia Robinson was also the first woman mathematician to be honored with election to the National Academy of Sciences. She received a number of awards including a Mac Arthur Foundation Prize and honorary doctorates.

FUN FACT:
Julia has a math festival named in her honor - the Julia Robinson Mathematics Festival

She was elected to the American Academy of Arts and Sciences; she was also given the presidency of the American Mathematical Society. This made her the first woman to hold this position of mathematical stature.

4) florence Nightingale: Statistician 1820 to 1910

To think of Florence Nightingale as merely a nurse is to do the lady a great injustice. Born into a privileged family, Florence Nightingale rejected the life of a society lady in order to pursue her passions for mathematics, statistics and greater public health.

Such was her passion for mathematics that she is quoted as saying that, she found the sight of a long column of figures "perfectly reviving". When the Crimean war began in 1853, Florence volunteered her services and was made Superintendent of the female nursing establishment in the English General Military Hospitals in Turkey and took a group of 38 nurses with her. On arrival, Florence was dismayed by the conditions of the hospitals and their documentation that she set out to do something about it. One of the first books Nightingale wrote, Notes on Matters Affecting Health, Efficiency, and Hospital Administration of the British Army (1858), provided statistical evidence that showed just how much of the mortality was due to the conditions of the hospitals. On the strength of her work, she was summoned by Queen Victoria to Balmoral the week after she returned from the Crimea.

FUN FACT:
In her 20s, Florence Nightingale rejected traditional Christianity and affirmed that she awaited the coming of a female Christ

She was keen to meet The Queen and Prince Albert, an emphatic supporter and patron of science and statistics, and she successfully procured their support for a Royal Commission on the health of the army.

5) Marjorie Lee Burke: Mathematics Educator 1914 to 1979

A graduate of Howard University, Marjorie Lee Browne overcame diversity in the form of racism to become one of the world's most renowned teachers and lecturers in mathematics.

In addition to joining the faculty at NCCU, Marjorie also works as a researcher and investigator and was lecturer for the Summer Institute for Secondary School Science and Mathematics Teachers. Ahead of her time, Marjorie saw the importance of computer science early on and wrote a $60,000 grant to IBM to bring a computer to NCCU in 1960—one of the first computers in academic computing, and almost certainly the first at a historically black school.

After her death, four of her students established the Marjorie Lee Browne Trust Fund at North Carol--- Central University which sponsors the Marjorie Lee Browne Scholarship r ..'c M.. .. ..c .ne Distinguished Alumni Lecture Series.

FUN FACT:
Marjorie Lee Browne won the Memphis city women's tennis singles championship when she was in high school

Marjorie was the first recipient of W. W. Rankin Memorial Award for Excellence in Mathematics Education, given by the North Carolina Council of Teachers in Mathematics.

Statistics in STEM

The US government has used the census to understand the American workforce. A new study published in 2018 gave the world insight into how woman are not well represented in the STEM fields. From the mid century to the new millennium there has been a definite increase in female scientists, but woman are still under represented in these fields. That simply wont do. There is a little girl right now who would grow up to cure cancer, explore a new galaxy or even discover a new type of energy. Let's inspire more awesome girls to share their point of you and make amazing discoveries!

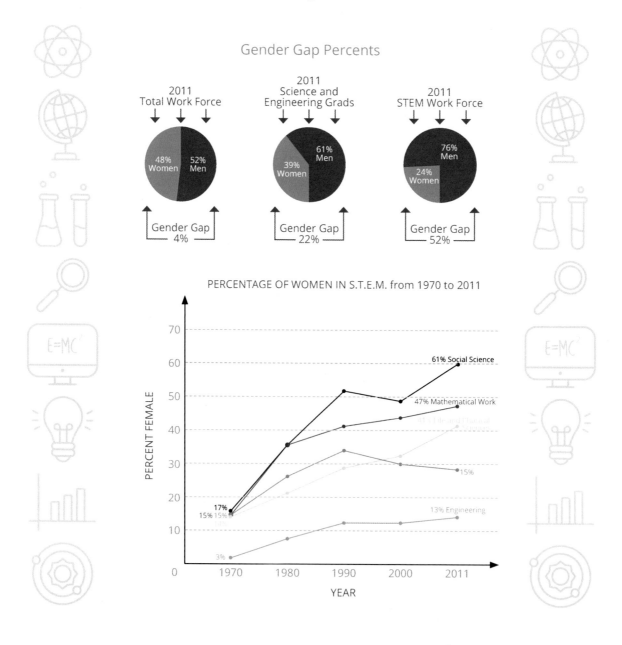

Gender Gap Percents

2011
Total Work Force

48% Women · 52% Men

Gender Gap 4%

2011
Science and Engineering Grads

61% Men · 39% Women

Gender Gap 22%

2011
STEM Work Force

76% Men · 24% Women

Gender Gap 52%

PERCENTAGE OF WOMEN IN S.T.E.M. from 1970 to 2011

PERCENT FEMALE

61% Social Science
47% Mathematical Work
15%
13% Engineering
17%
15% 15%
3%

YEAR

Join the

WIZKIDS CLUB

Enter today and win
a FREE BOOK!

Do you have any travel
adventure stories or project ideas
you want share with me? Yes?
Great! You can mail me at my id
and become a member of
the WIZKIDS CLUB!

www.wizkidsclub.com

Write to me at: sumita@wizkidsclub.com

Made in the USA
Columbia, SC
16 October 2020